Chasing Storms and Other Weather Disturbances

Weather for Kids

Children's Earth Sciences Books

BABY PROFESSOR

EDUCATION KIDS

Speedy Publishing LLC
40 E. Main St. #1156
Newark, DE 19711
www.speedypublishing.com

In this book, we're going to cover people who chase storms and other weather disturbances. So, let's get right to it!

WHO ARE STORM CHASERS?

Imagine you see a deadly tornado coming straight toward you. What would you do? Most people would drive away or go down into a basement to hide and ride out the storm, but there are a few people who do just the opposite. They go straight into the path of the dangerous oncoming storm! These people are fearless and they love storms.

Storm chasers pursue tornadoes and thunderstorms. They're fascinated with these storms and want to see them up close. Instead of being afraid of thunder, lightning and hail, chasers are excited by witnessing these storms.

They enjoy observing the towering vertical cumulonimbus clouds that storms create. Some chasers go after cyclones in the tropics and also waterspouts, forms of tornadoes that travel over water. They think that storms are exciting and beautiful works of nature and they want to be part of witnessing their fury.

WHY DO STORM CHASERS DO WHAT THEY DO?

There are lots of reasons why storm chasers enjoy following and observing storms. Some people like to get great photographs or videos of the storm. Chasers enjoy the exciting views of both sky and land during a storm. Others like the excitement of not knowing what will happen next.

This is particularly true when following tornadoes since they can change direction quickly. Some chasers love the feeling of the wide expanses of road and the feeling that they are participating in the greater natural world. Some chasers love the challenge of predicting where the storm will go next and finding the perfect spot to watch it.

Some chasers love the competitive excitement of being the first to get to a storm. There's also a social aspect of this "sport" since people who have a similar interest in storms meet up when they get there.

Scientists chase storms too. The study of weather is called meteorology and budding meteorologists are frequently involved in government or university projects to gather data about storms. There's a special Air Force Team called the Hurricane Hunters who fly into hurricanes and other tropical storms to report their observations.

WHAT IS A STORM SPOTTER?

Some observers look for approaching storms and report them to the appropriate authorities at the National Weather Service or local emergency management. These people are called storm spotters. The government organization called SKYWARN has a network of volunteer spotters who communicate through amateur radio operators and the internet. Reports from spotters have saved many lives since spotting was started in the 1940s.

These up-to-the-minute warnings are very helpful in ensuring that the public is aware when a storm is turning deadly. The data collected from advance spotting of storms is used in databases for studying climate and weather forecasting. Both storm chasers and storm spotters provide up-close photos as well as videos that are useful to researchers and the National Weather Service.

You don't have to have any specific educational background to be a storm chaser. There is some training available for storm spotters. In the springtime, the National Weather Service holds classes and workshops for people who want to become storm spotters and SKYWARN offers a certification for spotters.

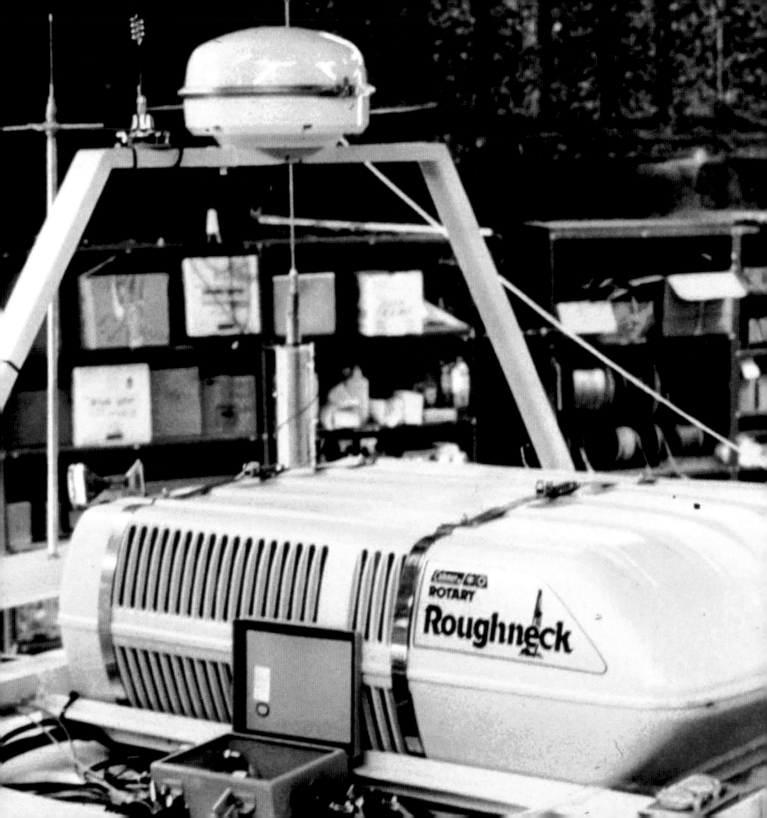

CAN YOU GET PAID TO BE A STORM CHASER?

It's expensive to chase storms. In some cases, you have to burn up gas driving great distances to get to a location that's ideal for witnessing a severe storm.

Very few people make money as storm chasers. Some television and media crews are paid to televise the storm. Photographers and videographers sometimes make money from dramatic still or moving images of storms.

A few "storm chase tour" services have started where tourists are taken out to a storm location by an individual or individuals who have experience as storm chasers, but these businesses are expensive to run and make little profit.

WHO BECOMES A STORM CHASER?

Storm chasers come from all walks of life. Many are located in the central and southern United States since there are so many thunderstorms and tornadoes in that area. A sizable number have some training in meteorology, but most storm chasers have no educational background in studying weather. The average age of a storm chaser is mid-thirties, but there are teenage storm chasers and also people in their 70's. No matter what they do as a regular job, storm chasers love nature in all its forms.

HISTORY OF STORM CHASING

A well-educated sketch artist and photographer, David Hoadley began chasing storms in North Dakota in the 1950's. He's known as the first storm chaser. He founded a magazine about chasing storms called Storm Track magazine. Hoadley is a detailed record keeper. He taught himself all about meteorology. He's driven over 750,000 miles and witnessed over 200 tornadoes in his pursuit of storms.

Another important storm chaser was Neil B. Ward. He worked throughout the 1950's and 1960's and persuaded the Oklahoma Highway Patrol to cooperate with him in researching storms.

The University of Oklahoma and the National Severe Storms Laboratory launched the Tornado Intercept Project in 1972. It was the first chase that was undertaken by a learning institution to get data about tornadoes. By this time, storm chasers had banded together over their common interest and kept connected through Hoadley's Storm Track magazine.

From the 1970's through the 1990's, storm chasing became a focus in popular culture. Some documentaries gave an accurate picture of what storm chasing was all about but others, like the movie Twister, kept all the Hollywood drama but left out the long drives and tiring waiting periods.

A TYPICAL STORM CHASE

Storm chasers sometimes have to drive thousands of miles to get to a location where they can witness an active storm or tornado. Some days they get to the location and nothing happens. Some chasers spend a lot of time forecasting before they hit the road so they can minimize down time. They also use weather data information on their travels to figure out how to get closer to the storm faster. Since so many storm chasers are not meteorologists, many of them are self- taught and learn a lot about weather as their "hobby" gets more and more addictive.

Despite the dramatic Hollywood view of the life of a storm chaser, most of the chaser's time is spent driving sometimes in very hazardous conditions, and waiting, waiting and more waiting. During the wait times, chasers review weather data, visit nearby landmarks or get together to play pickup sports.

Sometimes it looks like a storm is going to happen but then the clouds disappear and the storm doesn't "fire," which essentially means it doesn't start. On the other hand, when a tornado or other severe storm is happening, there's no time to eat or even to go to the bathroom! You've got to follow the storm to be where the action is happening and there's no time to lose.

DANGERS OF STORM CHASING

As you can imagine, if you're heading straight into a tornado, bad things can happen. In 2013, a tragic accident happened when a tornado in Oklahoma made an unexpected turn killing three men who were very experienced chasers.

Despite this, chasers are rarely killed by weather hazards. In most cases, tornadoes only affect limited areas and there are strategies that chasers can use to avoid high risk. They can maintain a safe distance and make sure they have an open escape route. They can also avoid traveling in the direction the tornado is traveling.

In the Northern Hemisphere, tornadoes generally travel from southwest to northeast or from west to east. Lightning is a very real danger as is heavy rain. Storm chasers have a slang phrase for driving through an area with intense rain. They call it "core punching."

Driving is very hazardous during core punching because the rain is so heavy you can't see. Another slang phrase they use is the "bear's cage." This phrase means the rotating thunderstorm that is wrapped in rain and could have a tornado at its center.

Not only is there the hazard of a hidden tornado, there's also very large hail, sometimes as big as baseballs. Anyone who decides to brave the "bear's cage" has to be lucky to get out alive.

Surprisingly, the most hazardous part of being a storm chaser is the driving especially when a lot of other storm chasers are on the road at the same time. As storm chasing increases in popularity, chasers fill up the roads, causing dangerous conditions. When roads are clogged up, people can't get out fast, so if a storm takes a turn, there's no way to get out.

Storm chasers call this type of traffic tie up "chaser convergence." When chasers push the limits of safety, they cause dangerous conditions for themselves as well as others who live and work in the area of severe storms.

Now you know more about chasing storms and why people do it. You can find more Earth Science books from Baby Professor by searching the website of your favorite book retailer.

Visit

BABY PROFESSOR
EDUCATION KIDS

www.BabyProfessorBooks.com

to download Free Baby Professor eBooks and view
our catalog of new and exciting Children's Books